LISTEN TO NATURE
Living in Harmony with the Earth

Sri Chinmoy (1931-2007) was a spiritual teacher, poet, philosopher, musician and athlete who dedicated his life to the pursuit of an integral vision of peace and harmony in the individual and the world. The recipient of numerous awards, he has been recognised globally for the simplicity and hope-affirming power of his work. Born in India, he made his home in New York City from 1964 until his passing in 2007.

Love of Nature permeated his inner experiences from an early age and was expressed in his poetry and other writings. In 1970 he began offering non-denominational Peace Meditations for delegates and staff at the United Nations, at the invitation of Secretary-General U Thant. For over thirty years, as he met to share inspiration with many dignitaries and seekers, he often responded to their concerns and questions about the environmental crisis, offering his perspective on humanity's relationship with the natural world as well as the role of science and technology. He viewed respect for Nature as an inseparable part of the overarching vision of peace. His illumining views on these crucial issues have been collected in this volume.

Praise for Sri Chinmoy

"It is a very rare gift indeed for humankind to be blessed with such a selfless individual who has dedicated his entire life to the service of world peace.... Your work has inspired spiritual growth, resilience and well-being, especially in view of the present and unprecedented onslaughts against humankind.... Yours is a voice of reason that we must all heed."

— PRESIDENT NELSON MANDELA

"Your deeds are invaluable, for they cannot be measured by any economic or political parameters. They are noble and cure the human soul."

— PRESIDENT MIKHAIL GORBACHEV

"We are each a pool of love, compassion and serenity. Let the ripples from this pool reach to the end of the world. This is what my dear friend Sri Chinmoy did, throughout his life, for all of God's children. God is smiling to know the immense good he has accomplished while working tirelessly to unite us all."

— ARCHBISHOP DESMOND TUTU

"Sri Chinmoy is an extraordinary peace innovator whose initiatives are founded upon humanity's common values and the vision that we are all members of one human family. He has empowered large numbers of people to participate in building harmony in their own lives, communities and nations."

— PROFESSOR ARNE NAESS
Founder of deep ecology

Listen *to* Nature

LIVING IN HARMONY WITH THE EARTH

Selected writings and talks by

Sri Chinmoy

Listen to Nature –
She speaks
Only for your good.

 Sri Chinmoy

ISBN 978-3-89532-337-9

Bird drawings by Sri Chinmoy
Back cover photo by Ranjana Ghose

Published by The Golden Shore Publishing House
Spreestraße 4, 44143 Dortmund, Germany
www.goldenshore.de

Distributed in North America by Heart-Light Publications, Seattle
www.heart-light.com

Printed in the Czech Republic

Acknowledgements

Much gratitude to Dr. Jane Goodall for her inspiration and support, and for kindly contributing her Foreword.

Many thanks to those who helped compile or review the text in this volume, including: Dr. Kusumita Pedersen (for her Introduction as well), Dr. Thomas Pliske, Dr. Ram Fishman, Natabara Rollosson, Sanjay Rawal and Begabati Lennihan.

�֍

Special thanks to Ranjana K. Ghose, President of the Board of Trustees, Sri Chinmoy Centre, New York, and Curator of the Jharna-Kala Art Foundation, for her dedication to Sri Chinmoy's writings and artwork celebrating the beauty and divinity of the natural world. ℘

CONTENTS

Foreword

THE WISDOM OF SRI CHINMOY, presented in this collection of his writing, is timely. He stresses the need for a deep spiritual connection with the natural world of which we are a part and on which we depend. For only when we learn to respect and live in harmony with nature can we hope to live in peace and harmony with each other. It is our disrespect of the natural world and animals that created the Covid-19 pandemic and has also led to the twin threats of biodiversity loss and climate change. Let us heed the words of this spiritual teacher before it is too late.

JANE GOODALL, PhD, DBE
Founder of the Jane Goodall Institute
and UN Messenger of Peace

Introduction

SRI CHINMOY BECAME KNOWN during his lifetime
(1931-2007) as the exponent of a dynamic spirituality
of transformation, by which both the individual and
society transcend their limitations and grow into greater
perfection. He advocated acceptance of the world
with love and concern, affirming the duty of service to
humanity – and indeed to all living beings as forms of the
Divine. Our dedicated action, guided by spiritual values,
devoted to the common good and based on the foundation
of meditation and prayer, is essential for this transformation.
This includes protecting the natural world and solving
environmental problems, as aspects of a global crisis in
which everything is interconnected.

This is the first book to collect from Sri Chinmoy's extensive writings in poetry and prose passages concerning our relation to Nature. Many of these are answers to questions, others are from lectures and a great many are poems that directly express the vision and insight arising from his profound spiritual realization. We hope that his words will cast light on the deeper causes of our present crisis and offer hope and inspiration as we take practical action with spiritual commitment.

Sri Chinmoy was born and raised in the 1930s in the rural village of Shakpura on the southern bank of the Karnaphuli River in the Chittagong region of East Bengal. It was an area of great natural beauty, where the river runs west down from the mountains of the Chittagong Hill Tracts to form the wide and deep harbour of the ancient multi-cultural port city of Chittagong. He was the youngest of seven children in a well-educated and prosperous Hindu family. As a child, he was allowed to roam freely in the meadows, groves and forests of the unspoiled countryside. His intimate communion with Nature began at this time and continued during his twenty years on the

Sri Aurobindo Ashram in Pondicherry on the shore of the Bay of Bengal, where he lived from age twelve to thirty-two. There he spent countless hours in meditation and soon experienced inner illumination and God-union which was ever-deepening, as he has recounted in his writings; this realization became the foundation of his lifework for peace and a better world.

The poetry that he wrote prolifically beginning in his teens is permeated by the imagery of Nature: the sun, moon and stars, the ocean, rivers that flow and reach the sea, flowers, trees that grow from a seed, blossom and bear fruit, dawn, evening and the flight of birds. In this poetry we see vividly that all beings in the natural world have a soul and their own personhood. Each in its own way knows that it comes from a supreme Source. Each rejoices in its interrelation with all others in God's vast creation, in the beauty of the world and the divine Presence in everything. Selections from Sri Chinmoy's poetry which express joy in the beauty of Nature and the delight of cosmic communion have been chosen for this book as expressing an indispensable dimension of our spiritual experience.

In his writings Sri Chinmoy consistently says that God, the one Absolute, "becomes" the universe, and therefore everything that exists in Nature is God in another form, as the One has become the Many. The purpose of this becoming is the divine Play or *Līlā*, in which there is an ever-increasing joy in the experience of multiplicity and diversity. The world is not an illusion but is real because it is the Body of God, and as such the world must be accepted and cared for with love and concern. There is always a distinction between the transcendent and the universal, but both are modes of the divine Reality. As Sri Chinmoy says, "In His transcendent aspect, / God is the Lord of Nature. / In His universal aspect, / God is Nature itself."* Many key passages that articulate the main points of Sri Chinmoy's understanding of Nature have been included in this collection to present his philosophy, with its richness, depth and subtlety, in his own words.

Every single being in the created world has its own unique inherent value and is boundlessly loved by God, its

* Sources of Sri Chinmoy's writings are shown on page 134.

Creator. We should likewise love our fellow beings in the universe and devote ourselves to them. Sri Chinmoy very often uses the expressions "God the Creator" and "God the creation." Ultimately they are indivisible and we should love and serve them as one: "We must serve / God the creation / Exactly the way we love / God the Creator." As he also says, "God the Creator / Loves you. / God the creation / Needs you. / To God the Creator / Give your heart. / To God the creation / Give your life."

Sri Chinmoy further affirms that the universe is evolving, in a process of unfolding the "involved" or immanent divine qualities present from the beginning, bringing forth divine qualities such as Light, Love, Beauty and Peace more and more into the external world over many ages. He calls this evolutionary transformation, which is both spiritual and physical, "God-manifestation." As human beings we should participate consciously in this cosmic progress through our aspiration – a longing for a better and higher life, often spoken of as a spiritual hunger or a flame within our heart. Meditation and prayer as well as dedicated service play an essential role in the life of aspiration, as Sri Chinmoy explains in these pages. In meditation we can open ourselves to the beauty of Nature, which lifts us up and illumines us, and also gives us strength and insight to take the actions needed to engage the environmental crisis.

He most often describes the overarching goal of this transformation and world-service as "Peace." Since ancient times the meaning of "Peace" in various traditions has been wholeness and has embraced not only the absence of conflict or an inner serenity, but also healing and the harmony of the entire outer and inner world. Many prayers from the Veda, the oldest scripture of Hinduism, end with an invocation of Peace or Shanti: "Aum, Shanti, Shanti, Shanti." One of the best known of all Vedic prayers is the Shanti Mantra (*Yajur Veda 36.17*), which invokes peace throughout the natural world and spiritual realms. It follows below in Sri Chinmoy's own translation from Sanskrit:

May there be peace in Heaven.
May there be peace in the sky.
May there be peace on earth.
May there be peace in the water.
May there be peace in the plants.
May there be peace in the trees.
May there be peace in the gods.
May there be peace in Brahma.
May there be peace in all.

❧

Peace in its fullest sense can be described in the words of the Earth Charter, an international civil society declaration finalized in 2000: "Peace is the wholeness created by right relationships with oneself, other persons, other cultures, other life, Earth and the larger whole of which all are a part." Sri Chinmoy states that peace is not merely the absence of conflict and tension; "Real peace is the unmistakable establishment of celestial harmony and universal Love."

His vision of peace is integral and inclusive and embraces humans in relation to each other, our relation with Nature and also Nature in itself in its own dignity and worth.

In the immense journey of Earth through hundreds of millions of years, human beings have appeared only in the last few moments. Yet we have already become a force with impact on a planetary scale, diminishing and damaging the very systems of Mother Earth that sustain us and all other living beings. As is now widely recognized, the root causes of this destruction are spiritual. According to Sri Chinmoy they lie in human ignorance – in aggression, fear, greed and the desire for supremacy. These are located especially in the "division-mind" and the mind's impulse to dominate, as ignorance in a spiritual sense means separateness, a not knowing the oneness or unity-in-diversity of all existence. While we must swiftly take all possible necessary action to end the global crisis, Sri Chinmoy affirms that lasting peace among people and enduring harmony with Nature will only be established through transformation effected by spiritual practice and aspiration relying on the love-power of the heart.

No matter how grave the harm may be, because Nature is God's creation, what has been damaged or destroyed can be over time healed, regenerated and restored by its Creator. We should participate in this restoration not only by our outer actions but also through our inner aspiration invoking God's help in the healing of the Earth. This is a message of hope urging us to both constructive action and meditative practice in the present crisis of global ecological devastation and climate change. As we act outwardly, our prayer and meditation can play an essential role in deepening our love and respect for Nature and our oneness with Nature, other human beings and all life.[*]

KUSUMITA P. PEDERSEN
Professor Emerita of Religious Studies
St. Francis College
April 2021

[*] This final paragraph is drawn from Kusumita P. Pedersen, "Sri Chinmoy's Philosophy of Nature." *Journal of Dharma Studies,* Vol. 4, No. 1 (April 2021). Special Issue on Ecotheology edited by Christopher Fici and Kenneth Valpey.

Editor's Preface

To MAKE SRI CHINMOY'S WRITINGS on Nature available to a wider audience has been a long-cherished dream for many of those involved in producing this volume.

In my thirty years working at the United Nations, where I served as a communications strategist and media spokesperson on sustainable development issues, I saw first-hand the political difficulties of building consensus and action on the serious environmental problems we face. I also have long appreciated Sri Chinmoy's wisdom and philosophy of peace, which he offered to the UN community from

1970 until his passing in 2007. Twice weekly he would hold silent meditations for peace, and on occasion also offer talks and answer questions from delegates and staff; some of these exchanges are captured in this volume. Along with many colleagues, I felt that his spiritual perspective offers insight and inspiration, even as the UN's Sustainable Development Goals have brought greater attention to how the environment and sustainability are interconnected with all global aims for peace and development.

I also witnessed how hopelessness and despair are growing in the environmental movement, especially among a new generation of climate activists who are hearing from scientists that time is running out to make the transformations needed if we are to avoid the calamities that seem more and more inevitable. The Covid-19 pandemic has also brought to light the impacts of our severe imbalance with the natural world, adding to the concern that perhaps we are already reaping the karmic fruits of our wanton destruction of natural habitats.

Sri Chinmoy's message is one of hope. From his deep insight, he reassures us that, even at this stage when so much damage has been done, the natural world can rebound, and we are already seeing glimpses of this regenerative phenomenon. He urges that a spiritual transformation is needed, on the individual and eventually global levels, to build the foundation for a sustainable human society that exists in harmony with the natural world.

We hope that these words will serve as an inspiration for all concerned citizens in tackling the enormous challenges that lie ahead.

PRAGATI PASCALE
New York, April 2021

The sky calls me,
The wind calls me,
The moon and stars call me.

The green and dense groves call me,
The dance of the fountain calls me,
Smiles call me, tears call me.
A faint melody calls me.

The morn, noon and eve call me.
Everyone is searching for a playmate,
Everyone is calling me, "Come, come!"
One voice, one sound, all around.
Alas, the Boat of Time sails on.

W hen life is really a question,
The answer can be found
In the natural beauty
Of Mother Earth.

Nature's Beauty:
A Source of Peace

NATURE HAS ITS OWN RHYTHM, its own harmony, its own peace and its own joy. When you are identified, consciously or unconsciously, with universal Nature, it is all vastness and immensity. There you lose your own outer existence, the existence of separateness, the feeling that you are separate from other persons. In that state of unified oneness, you become totally one with universal Nature; you become part and parcel of the vast and the Infinite. There you forget your ordinary life, which is your name, your physical frame and your outer existence. Indeed, this is a wonderful experience! In that state, you do not have to make your mind calm and quiet, for your mind itself is not functioning; you have already become identified with the treasure of universal Nature's consciousness. ೭

If peace is not
In Nature's beauty,
Then where is it, where?

Mother Earth,
Your beauty is unimaginable!
You are far beyond the appreciation
Of my heart and my life.

My heart adores
The simplicity-beauty
Of Mother Earth.

Nature's beauty helps us
To be as vast as possible,
As peaceful as possible
And as pure as possible.

❉

Nature's beauty
Teaches optimism
To the aspiring heart.

❉

Nature willingly
Wants to offer us
Its hidden ecstasy.

The best way to appreciate Nature's beauty is to sit and meditate with Nature. If you take a tree as Nature, then sit at the foot of a tree and meditate. If you take the sun as an expression of Nature, then look at the sun and meditate. If you feel the ocean or sea as Nature, then sit in front of the water and meditate. While looking at the tree or the sun or the ocean, try to feel your oneness with it. Anything that you consider as Nature or Nature's beauty, you should try to become one with.

Again, if you want a particular thing from Nature, you have to go to that thing. If you want to have vastness, then just go out of the house and look at the sky and you will enter into vastness. If you want to have a very vast, pure consciousness, then stand in front of a river and meditate on the river. And if you want to get height in your life, then go to a mountain and meditate there.

If you want to meditate on the power aspect of life, then look at the sun and meditate. The sun represents power, not the power that destroys, but the power that creates, originates. And if you want to have mildness, softness, tenderness in your life, then you can meditate on the moon.

So whatever you want, you have to stand in front of that particular thing and invoke it. You have to invoke the spirit of Nature or become one with the soul of Nature. That is the best kind of identification. ૨૦

Those who are more in tune with Mother Nature develop intuition. Through prayer and meditation, we can also develop intuition. And again, by loving Mother Earth, by loving a flower, loving a leaf, loving a tree, loving the water, loving Nature's beauty, we can develop intuition.

If it is difficult for you to develop intuition through prayer and meditation, only appreciate the beauty of the flowers, the beauty of the grass. If you can identify yourself with the beauty aspect of Nature, then you will develop intuition. ૨૦

The morning smile
Of Nature
Thrills my heart.

❋

The evening smile
Of Nature
Purifies my mind.

⚝ Meditation:
The Vastness of the Sky

Kindly keep your eyes half open and imagine the vast sky.
In the beginning try to feel that the sky is in front of you;
later try to feel that you are as vast as the sky, or that you
are the vast sky itself. After a few minutes, please close
your eyes and try to see and feel the sky inside your heart.
Please feel that you are now the Universal Heart, and that
inside you is the sky that you meditated upon and identified
yourself with. Your heart is infinitely vaster than the sky, so
you can easily house the sky within yourself. ೭

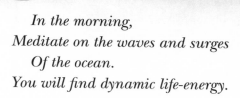

In the morning,
Meditate on the waves and surges
 Of the ocean.
You will find dynamic life-energy.

In the evening,
Meditate on the deep vastness
 Of the ocean.
You will feel Infinity's peace.

*E*ach beautiful flower
Is indeed a lovely letter
From God Himself
To mankind.

Silence embraces
Nature's beauty
   Most powerfully.

   The sweet whispers
      Of Mother Nature
   Awaken and enlighten me.

We can have
   Harmony
If we have
   A deep reverence
For Mother Nature.

One atom
Is equal to
The whole universe.

❋

No atom
Is empty of
God's Will.

❋

Beauty non-pareil has blossomed
In the heart of
The subtle atom-tapestry.

Nature embodies the cosmic energy
That leads us to the ultimate Source
While fulfilling us and satisfying us.

When we sit at the foot of a tree,
It shelters us with love.
He who is really great
Gives away all that he has and is for others.
The Seers and the Yogis leave their homes
And go and sit at the foot of the trees.
They find in the trees their true friends.
We must try to love all human beings
In the world of Light
As a tree loves us.

Meditation: The Compassion of a Tree

To develop compassion, meditate on a tree. Although the flowers, leaves and branches are above the ground, they are not looking downward with contempt or a feeling of superiority. The trunk of the tree may be very tall; the flowers, fruits and leaves may all be above us. But when we pass below the tree, the leaves, flowers and fruits say, "Take us; we are ready to be utilised by you." Because of its oneness with us, everything that is good and beautiful that the tree has, it is begging us to take.

Many large and old trees are deeply conscious of their existence. The tree is rooted in the ground, and at the same time it is trying to reach the sky. Like that, we shall live here in this world while our aspiration-flame climbs to the highest. The tree shows us how to remain firmly rooted on earth while going high, higher, highest.

We must be aware of
The nature of trees:
Sacrifice, sacrifice, sacrifice –
From the very foot
To the highest height.

*T*he heart of Mother Earth
Is full of tears.

❋

The sorrows
Of the earth-planet
I am.

The Tears
of Mother Earth:
The Roots of the
Environmental Crisis

NATURE'S PRISTINE BEAUTY must be preserved. Whenever or wherever we torture Mother Earth, we must feel that we have committed a serious crime. Nature's beauty and purity we must preserve.

Nature and heart go perfectly together. Right now we are using too much of the mind and not enough of our hearts. The mind has to be used; otherwise, we shall act foolishly. But the mind that we are using now is the doubting mind, suspicious mind, impure mind. Instead, let us use our heart of beauty, heart of purity, heart of divinity. This heart is always at one with Mother Nature, the Nature that gives us affection, compassion, love and blessings.

The things that Mother Nature has produced here on earth are beautiful. But we have become commercial. While we are modernising the whole world with our technological capacities, we are destroying the inner beauty and simplicity which Mother Earth embodies. This is an act of unpardonable stupidity and callousness. We are actually limiting ourselves in the name of transforming or improving Mother Earth.

There should be a balance. From Nature we can take as much help as we need, but always without diminishing Mother Earth's pristine beauty and capacity. ꕥ

Mother Earth,
My heart breaks into
Millions of pieces
The moment I think of
Your insufferable agonies.

God's creation unmistakably knows
That ruthless exploitation
Is the order of the day.

❋

Nature's message to mankind:
Do not kill me!
God will bless you
With His Compassion-Eye
And Forgiveness-Heart.

Mother Earth
Has to be treated
With utmost humility.

Remember –
Earth is God's Body.
Be extremely careful and soulful.

We must water
Mother Earth
With our heart's
Utmost reverence.

How do you feel about all the environmental concerns that seem to be surfacing now?

The very nature of earth is to cry, cry for purification. First it starts with a cry for simplicity, because earth has been polluted by complexity. Previously, hundreds and thousands of years ago, earth was very simple. Now human beings have corrupted the earth. On the one hand, machinery and technology have helped the earth considerably, but on the other hand, they have considerably taken away the pristine beauty, purity and divinity of Mother Earth. As soon as I see the soul of the earth, I see the soul is crying and crying because of the loss of its inner divinity, which is far, far greater than the gain in outer achievements. Earth has lost many, many divine qualities which it had from the beginning of creation.

The very nature of Mother Earth is to cry. One kind of cry is aspiring to become inseparably one with God the Creator. But at the same time earth has another cry to regain the invaluable things that it has lost over the centuries.

What is your opinion about the pollution of the environment?

It is a very sad thing that Nature is being polluted, that the environment is being destroyed. It is Nature that keeps us beautiful and soulful. When Nature is destroyed, when artificial things replace the natural beauty, it will ruin all the good qualities that human beings have. Unfortunately, people like artificial things, glamorous things. Many people do not like natural things, which have their own beauty, purity and divinity. I feel that we should pray that Nature should remain natural. The beauty of Nature should remain always as it is so that we can derive from it our purest joy, purest love and purest oneness.

Why is humanity polluting and destroying Mother Nature?

Mother Nature is being polluted and destroyed by the unaspiring realities of life. It is very sad. Mother Nature has become so helpless, and so many people who say they are trying to preserve Mother Nature are in no way helping. They are only talking, talking, talking!

Governments also are only talking. They come forward and say, "Yes, we want to preserve Mother Nature, the trees and fields," but their actions produce the opposite effect.

Because we human beings see enemies all around us, because we are afraid someone will come and attack us, we use all our money and energy to make ourselves powerful. To make ourselves powerful enough to fight our enemies, we cut Mother Nature into pieces and take her resources. We give importance only to scientific advancement, which does not allow Mother Nature to remain beautiful or powerful.

As long as there is fear on earth, Mother Nature will never be able to fulfil her divinity. It is only when we no longer see others as enemies that we shall be able to keep Mother Nature intact. ৯

Nature compassionately takes
Very little from us.
But we are always eager to devour
Not only everything from Nature
But also Nature itself.

❈

Do not underestimate
The blessing-gifts
Of Mother Earth.

❈

Mother Earth asks us
To follow her
And give everything
Cheerfully and unreservedly.

The following two questions were asked by Hanne Strong at a meeting that Sri Chinmoy had with her and her husband, Maurice Strong, while Mr. Strong was serving as Secretary-General of the 1992 United Nations Conference on Environment and Development (Earth Summit).

❊

The degradation of the earth is so far advanced right now that we may have already crossed the line of no return regarding the oceans, the soil and the forests. What is your opinion?

If we start doing the right thing, the earth can always start making progress again. Sometimes it happens that there are no plants in a garden. But when a most skilful gardener begins working there, once again the garden will start producing most beautiful plants, flowers, trees and fruits.

But if the soil is dead, it is dead. If a forest is gone, it is gone. If the ozone is gone, it is gone.

We must not underestimate the power of spirituality. Prayer and meditation mean new life. When we pray and meditate, at every second we are invoking God's Compassion. We are saying that Mother Nature is being destroyed. But we have to know that Mother Nature is nothing other than God the creation. We are praying to God the Creator to save God the creation. So He who created this earth can once again create a new creation on the strength of our prayers and meditations. ॐ

What we need is a life of balance — neither to wallow in the pleasures of wealth nor to lead a life of asceticism, but to embrace a life of simplicity and a heart of purity. Indeed, this is the only way that this world of ours can be supremely happy and divinely perfect. ☙

Nature is never spent.
Nature's beauty,
Nature's capacity,
Nature's reality,
Never run short of
God's infinite sea
And infinite sky.

About God: Author's Note

I believe in God. Other seekers will say that they believe
in Truth. My God and their Truth are identical. Still
others believe in Light. The Lord Buddha believed in
Light; he did not believe in God at all. His inner Light is
the same as our God. God and Light cannot be separated.
God and Truth cannot be separated. Again, if you have a
strong belief in yourself, then your own belief is the same
as my God. God can be Light, God can be Truth and God
can be belief, a very strong belief, for which we use the
term 'faith'.

God is addressed in various ways, according to one's
sweetest, most affectionate feeling. Instead of using the
word 'God', I use the word 'Supreme' most of the time.
When we say 'Supreme', we are speaking of the Supreme
Lord who not only reaches the absolute Highest, but all the
time goes beyond, beyond, and transcends the Beyond.

God is both masculine and feminine. The Christ always called God the Father, so the term 'Father' is more commonly used in the Western world. In the East, we quite often speak of the Supreme Goddess. Each Indian family has a presiding deity, and my family's presiding deity is the goddess Kali, Mahakali. I am extremely fond of her, and she has helped me many times. But when I am with Westerners, I use the term which is more familiar to you, because I feel that it will be easier for me to share my experiences with you in that way.

Nevertheless, God is both masculine and feminine. He is what He eternally is: He is His Vision and He is His Reality. This Reality embodies both masculine and feminine and also transcends both.

What is Nature? Nature is God the Mother. In God's masculine aspect, God is Transcendental. In God's feminine aspect, God is Universal. ℘

The following question was asked by Mary Evelyn Tucker, co-director and co-founder of the Yale Forum on Religion and Ecology and Senior Lecturer and Research Scholar, School of the Environment, Divinity School, and Department of Religious Studies, Yale University.

※

In the light of the current environmental crisis, how would you see God in Nature?

God the Creator and God the creation are one. Nature is the outer expression of God. The environmental crisis that we are seeing at present, especially in the twentieth century, may take away some beauty from Nature, or we can say her beauty may be partially destroyed, but the inner divinity of Nature or the environment can never be destroyed.

Nature is God's revelation and manifestation. God is Nature's Source. You can say that Nature is God in His outer Form. When a crisis in the environment takes place, we may lose Nature's beauty but not Nature's divinity. Even when the ocean is polluted at various places, or when a forest is turned into a wasteland, we can never say that God has left the ocean or the forest. God will always remain inside both creation and destruction because He is beyond creation and destruction.

Hiroshima and Nagasaki were destroyed by atom bombs. Beauty left those two cities, but divinity remained. Now that divinity is expressing itself in the most soulful peace shrines that have been built in the ruins. The man-made power that is tempted to destroy the world will definitely be arrested by the Heart-Power of God.

Ignorant people who are destroying Nature will not remain ignorant forever. In this century, war-mongers have been successful in their destruction-attempts directed towards some countries. Again, peace-lovers with their superior wisdom are not allowing the war-mongers to succeed as freely as they did in the past.

The mind has destruction-power. The heart has creation-power and enlightenment-power. Today's doubting and destructive mind will grow into tomorrow's searching mind and creative heart. Today's matter-satisfaction-hunger will be turned into tomorrow's spirit-nourishment-meal.

The blind powers
Of the human mind
Cannot forever rule the world.

※

Mother Nature
Is the only God-creation-reality
That does not expect anything in return.
She just gives and gives unconditionally –
Unreservedly she gives,
With no expectation-hope.

Meditation: The Beauty of a Flower

Feel that you have entered into a garden with many, many flowers. Choose one flower that you like and go near it. Appreciate its beauty and smell its fragrance. Then just say a few times, "How I wish I could be as pure and as beautiful as this flower." After five minutes, try to imagine that an infinitesimal amount of beauty from that flower has entered into you. Then gradually try to feel that all the good qualities you are seeing in the flower – its beauty, its purity, its fragrance and so on – have entered into you and are inside you. Then try to feel that you do not have a body, you do not have a mind, you do not have anything. Think of yourself only as that most beautiful flower.

Sailing the boat of silver light,
The moon-beauty is fast approaching me.
The sky is vibrating with sweet and melodious songs.
The birds are flying beyond the horizon
To an unknown land.
All my hopes are flying without any destination.
Slowly my life's evening sets in.

*E*very self-giving effort
Of every human being
Is needed to change
The fate of this world.

The Transformation of the World:
What Each of Us Can Do

EACH INDIVIDUAL HAS A SPECIAL ROLE to play in the protection of our small planet. It is the illumination of the individual mind and spirit that will precede the awakening of a new collective awareness. The change in individual attitudes will be the precursor of a change in institutional policies, and the result will be a greater respect and love for our planet Earth.

Problems are everywhere. Each country has hundreds of problems. Each individual has hundreds of problems. But problems can be solved, should be solved and must be solved by individuals first. If each individual dives deep into his own countless problems, he comes to realise that there is only one problem, and that problem is lack of oneness. ༐

I am responsible
Not only for my own life,
But for the earth-planet as well.

The greatest mistake in life
Is to remain indifferent
To the world-situation.

God asks
Each and every one of us
To take good care of the world.

Will mankind survive the impending ecological disasters? How can our modern technological society be taught to respect our home, the planet Earth?

Mankind will survive everything precisely because God will not allow His perfection-manifestation on earth to be a failure. But it is very difficult to impress upon others the necessity of respecting and preserving our Mother Earth. Everybody has to be taught through inner persuasion and outer example.

Inner persuasion has to be founded upon our prayers and meditations. Those who are conscious of higher ideals have to pray to God and meditate on God to illumine the destruction-thirsty minds of the world and transform them into perfection-longing minds. Also, we have to pray to God and meditate on God to create and develop a genuine universal oneness-hunger in the life of humanity.

The development of technology is not bad in itself. But we have to see whether technology is utilised for the divine satisfaction of mankind or for man's mutual self-destruction. Our planet Earth, which God has chosen for His complete manifestation, will be inundated with light and delight when we all live in our purity-heart-garden and not in our impurity-mind-jungle. ⌒

Over-population is not good; pollution is not good. But why are they happening? Because people are ignorant. We have to go to the root cause of world problems, and the root is human ignorance. If we can go to the root and remove this ignorance in just one human being — ourselves — then there will be one rascal less in this world. Today if there is one rascal less, tomorrow there may be another rascal less, and in this way it will go on. When I become good, automatically there is one more positive force and one less negative force on earth. If I can transform my own ignorance into light, then the quantity of ignorance on earth has already decreased. ⌒

Each human being is expected to be
        A soulful ambassador of goodwill
To improve the standard of mankind.

❈

        To change one's life
            Is to increase
        The world-transformation-hopes.

❈

        To be of service,
    I give my loving heart
        To Mother Earth.

How does our aspiration affect the earth-environment?

Definitely our aspiration helps the environment. Some political figures speak about the environment twenty-four hours a day. Forgive me to say, how much conviction do they have in their own pronouncements? They say various places will be destroyed. Many years ago some religious figures said the world would be destroyed. We see darkness. It is very easy to see darkness, but where is the light? How shall we bring down light?

If I see darkness, then I must show the light also. If I only see darkness and I tell the world, "Bring light, bring light," am I going to achieve anything? If I have the capacity to see darkness, then I should also have the vision to bring down light. Otherwise, what shall I offer to the world? You see darkness and you tell the world, "My house is being destroyed." Are you taking care of it, or are you just depending on your neighbours to come and take care of your house?

The environment is like that. If we can improve the condition of the environment, it will be our own enlightenment. But unfortunately we see things, we talk about things, but we often do not have the remedy. We do not have the answer. We tell others to provide the medicine. We ourselves see the disease and the forthcoming result, but we may not have the medicine.

Again, some people do not even see the disease. The environment, for them, is perfect. If they do not see the disease, why should they care for a remedy? If I see the disease, then I should come forward with a cure. I cannot say that the remedy has to be provided by somebody else. No! If I see the disease, I should also come forward with the medicine. ꙮ

In the face of natural disasters, such as earthquakes and tsunamis, there are two ways in which we can respond. The first is to feel that human beings must respect Nature much more. The second is to feel that human beings should come first and so we need even more advanced technology to protect humans from disasters. Which is your view?

I most sincerely subscribe to both views. Firstly, we have to respect Nature. President Gorbachev* and others are trying desperately to save Mother Nature. Here, there, everywhere, Nature is being destroyed, so their Green Cross organisation and other groups are trying to preserve Nature, preserve the environment. Nature is the expression of our inner life, our higher life. It is from Nature that we get all good things—beauty, tranquillity, humility, simplicity and many other divine qualities. Above all, Nature is spontaneous. When we develop the mind, we become so

* Sri Chinmoy met numerous times and corresponded regularly with Soviet President Mikhail Gorbachev, who in 1993 co-founded the Green Cross, an international environmental organisation.

complex; we cannot do anything spontaneously. Nature helps us to regain our spontaneity. Like this, Nature helps us in millions of ways to become good citizens of the world. That is why we must respect and adore Nature.

Your second point is that we need even more advanced technology to protect humans from disaster. I also fully agree with this statement. Science and technology must make progress. But, forgive me to say, no matter how far we advance with our science and technology, if Nature becomes furious, Nature is not going to surrender to our scientific and technological achievements. The universal Nature is infinitely more powerful than the scientific achievements of man. These achievements, I tell you, will be no match for Mother Nature if she becomes furious.

So these are two approaches: advanced technology and our respect for Mother Nature so that she does not get angry with us and torture us by creating natural disasters and devastation. Your two approaches are absolutely right, but if I am allowed, I would like to add one more approach which will not interfere at all with the first two. This third approach is prayer — prayer to the highest, to the strongest, to the most powerful One to protect us from harm, from Nature's disasters, or from anything and anybody.

All three approaches should be combined — love of Nature, inner wisdom and the advancement of technology. Then we will be able to face Nature's disasters. Inner wisdom is nothing but love, the feeling of oneness. If we sincerely love someone, then that person is not going to harm us.

This world is only one family. You are my sister; I am your brother. Each individual in this family has something unique to contribute to the world at large. We can all live together peacefully or we can quarrel and fight and wage wars.

So this world of ours has two choices: one is to establish friendship, brotherhood and oneness. Another is to try to conquer or destroy others. When we adopt this approach, ultimately, we destroy ourselves.

If we can apply all three approaches at the same time, then there is a great possibility for us to avert Nature's disasters. ౼

God tells us
That we came into the world
Not to command Nature,
But to obey Nature.

❃

We came into the world
To fight for Mother Earth
Against her countless enemies.

❃

God does not want me
Just to feel sad
For the earth-planet.
He wants me to do something
To serve her
And make her smile and smile.

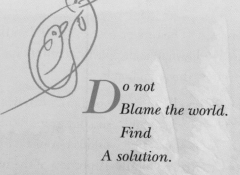

***D**o not
Blame the world.
Find
A solution.*

Many say that we are entering into the end of this age, and that the world is going to end quite soon. Is there going to be an end of the world?

The world is very vast. The universe is very vast. Nothing can totally destroy it. Human consciousness cannot be destroyed, not even by the atom bomb.

Since your childhood I am sure you have been hearing that the world is coming to an end. And our grandfathers were also told the same story. The world is not just a tiny spot. It will not be destroyed totally. A portion of the world may be destroyed by an earthquake or some cataclysm, but the whole world as such is not going to be destroyed. Human aspiration is not going to come to an end.

Human aspiration is like an upward movement. It goes up, then it bends a little and then again it goes up. Human aspiration may go up and down, ascend and descend, but ultimately it just goes up. If somebody becomes tired while he is climbing, then in his time of relaxation perhaps he comes down a little. But when he is again inspired, he will go up again and finally he will reach the Highest. The world is not going to come to an end because human aspiration is not going to come to an end. Human aspiration may one day be very hot and another day it may be lukewarm, but when it once starts in us, it will carry us to the highest Absolute. Before it reaches that Goal, it will not be satisfied. So long as human aspiration exists in the earth atmosphere, this world will never be totally destroyed.

This world will never end, because inside the world is God's own Vision, God's own Hope, God's own Promise. If a potter creates a few vessels, a mad animal may for no reason come and destroy some of the vessels. But the potter can easily create more. God is the Creator. At every second He can create a new world. The Supreme will not allow human beings to destroy the world. It is His creation, after all.

Thinking of the problems in the world, one has to wonder if we are really making progress.

The world is constantly evolving towards a higher standard of life. It is not moving in a straight line, but rather in a spiral. Therefore, at times this progress is not immediately noticeable. To our human mind it may seem confusing and baffling. But on the strength of our inner oneness with the world situation and world evolution, we can see unmistakably the world's slow and steady progress.

Sometimes when we are practising the long jump, we start running and then hesitate a little. So we go back again and take a longer running start. When we come to the board, we say, "Am I going to make the leap? Perhaps I will not be able to cover the distance." So we go back and take an even longer run. This time we do the jump and cover our distance. But if we had jumped the first time, definitely we would not have been able to cover the distance. ᖷ

The following question was asked by representatives of the Red Cross on 11 January 2005 in Beijing, China, when they met with Sri Chinmoy soon after the Indian Ocean tsunami that devastated South Asia.

❋

During this huge tsunami disaster, what kind of spirit would we need to face it?

We need a spirit of oneness. This disaster has in a very special way helped us to bring the world together. The world of division must go. The world of oneness must come forward.

We human beings have been doing many, many things wrong over the years. I do not wish to use the term 'punishment', but let us say that somebody is trying to illumine us. Mother Nature is illumining us in a very special way. She is saying, "Now wake up, wake up!" This world has to be inundated with peace, joy and harmony. This disaster is, to me, a blessing in disguise. Many, many people who did not previously care for the world have now brought forward their hearts. They have come together with utmost sympathy and a feeling of oneness. This world belongs to each and every human being. We exist not only for our little family, but for the big family, which is the world.

On the one hand, this is a great disaster. On the other hand, if we look at it from a different point of view, it has helped immensely to bring about the feeling of oneness. Outwardly, it seems like a severe, severe punishment. Inwardly, we feel it has helped immensely to prove to the world at large that we belong to one family. ౼

Oneness first,
   And then only
Can we take a giant step
Towards world-transformation.

❋

We go to Mother Nature
   To give us joy,
But when Mother Nature
   Is displeased with us,
We become utterly helpless.

❋

When the forces of Nature
   Become destructive,
We can overcome them
On the strength of our purity-prayer
   And divinity-meditation.

One theory is that everything is God's Will. Again, the forces of Nature can manifest themselves through hurricanes and all kinds of negative acts. Nature is good, but many times Nature does things that are extremely contrary to God's Will. Some things happen that are unexpected. They may not be God's Will. A tiny little boat is in a river or in the ocean, and immediately a cyclone comes and kills the passengers. Is it God's Will? No!

How can people have faith when we face so much suffering in the world?

The sufferings that the world is now facing are unbelievable. Because of this tsunami, thousands and thousands of people have been killed. In one sense, we can say that Mother Nature is displeased with human beings. If we are sincere, each and every person on earth will see how many wrong things he has done individually and how many wrong things we have done collectively — nationally and internationally.

Sometimes we do wrong things unconsciously; sometimes we do them deliberately. A little child, for example, is unconscious of the fire. When he stands in front of the fire, just because he is innocent, do you think the fire will not burn him? The very nature of fire is to burn the child. As human beings, we have to be very frank with ourselves, whether we have done everything that is good within our capacity. Then we will see that human beings have done many, many wrong things consciously, deliberately and maliciously. Why? To show our supremacy.

So you can say that this tsunami is Nature's revolt, Nature's revenge. Mother Nature is like a real mother. She sees that her children are quarrelling, fighting and destroying everything, so she strikes them. She wants them to be good, exemplary citizens of the world. It is farther than the farthest from her mind to destroy the earth. She is only punishing her children to some extent so that they will turn over a new leaf.

This tsunami has given us a devastating experience. Again, the leaders of so many countries have united together to help those places that were severely affected. Human beings have once more brought to the fore their sympathy, which was practically buried in oblivion. With our divine qualities, we can unite the world. Again, with our undivine qualities, we can destroy the world.

To come back to your question, how can we free ourselves from suffering? We have to first of all love others and establish the feeling of oneness with them. This oneness is based on our inner existence. When we truly sympathise with somebody, then we take away some of his suffering. Let us say somebody's mother has passed away. If you happen to be a close friend of that person and you go there to console him, then you definitely decrease his suffering. Because you are sharing the suffering, the members of the family do not suffer the full amount.

In the case of the tsunami disaster which has taken place, the sympathy that the entire world has shown has really helped humanity. By exercising its sympathetic heart, the world has considerably decreased the suffering of those affected.

Suffering is there, but we can share it by establishing our oneness with those who are suffering. Always we have to have the feeling of goodwill. If, in your suffering, I go to be of service to you and vice versa, then we decrease the suffering.

A day will come when there will be another way of conquering suffering, and that way will be through light. Human life is composed of darkness and light. Darkness wants to envelop us and destroy light; light wants not to destroy darkness, but to illumine it. In the outer world, there will always be suffering, but there is a way to diminish the suffering and that way is the way of oneness, the establishment of oneness. If we use our sympathetic heart, our feeling of oneness, then the suffering is lessened to a considerable degree.

The ultimate goal of this Mother Earth, this earth-planet, is not suffering; it is joy. We came from Heaven, which is all joy. Now, on this particular planet, we are sad, unhappy, miserable, and for that we have to take the blame to a great extent. But consciously if we can expand and extend our love, goodwill and feeling of oneness, plus if we can go deep within, then there will be much less suffering. The ultimate goal of every human being is happiness. We know that we came from Heaven, which is nectar-happiness, and we are now passing through a longer than the longest tunnel which is dark and unlit. But we feel that at the end of the tunnel, no matter how long it is, light will again be waiting for us, and that light is happiness.

How do you envision politics in the twenty-first century?

I believe that eventually politics has to surrender to spirituality and allow itself to be guided and led by spirituality. The situation now in the political world is like a blind man trying to lead someone who has very clear vision. People who have clear vision live in the heart; they are the ones who should lead the blind. But instead, the blind are the ones who are leading. Who are the blind? The blind are those who live in the mind at every moment.

The mind only knows how to divide and divide. But by dividing the world and separating reality into pieces, we can never get joy. Only by becoming one with the world can we get real joy. The mind is like a boxer. It is always trying to show its supremacy. All the time it is saying: "I am superior to you. I should be one step higher than you or one step ahead of you."

The voice of the heart is the voice of oneness. It says, "Wherever you are, I am also there. I am inside your heart and you are inside my heart." This kind of oneness-philosophy brings us an abiding joy that we can never get from the world of separation and conquest. Today the boxer will defeat his opponent and tomorrow some other boxer will defeat him. So where is the satisfaction?

The mind not only separates itself from others; it also doubts and suspects others. It may even doubt and suspect itself. Those who live in the heart, on the other hand, are all the time expanding. Today they love God; tomorrow they will love all humanity. If spiritual people get the opportunity to help mental people who are now in the political world, then there will be a different kind of politics — the politics of the heart. At that time, guidance will come from the heart and there will be no division; there will be only joy and satisfaction.

World-unity is of paramount importance. If all the countries join together for a positive common goal, the very act of their being together is something laudable. Only this approach will eventually save the world and the planet. ᨓ

*The love of the heart
Is the way
To world-transformation.*

*S*cience is desperately searching
For the cosmic key.
　　　Nature already has it.

Science, Nature and Spirituality:
Searching for the Cosmic Key

Science and modern life are simply indispensable to each other. The modern life is the eye; science is the power of vision. Spirituality and the future life of mankind will be indispensable to each other. The future life of mankind will be the fully awakened consciousness; and spirituality will be its guiding and fulfilling soul.

What should be the relation between science and spirituality? It should be a relation of mutual acceptance and true understanding. It is an act of folly on our part to expect the same truth, the same knowledge and the same power from both science and spirituality. We must not do that. Neither must we set up the same goal for science and spirituality.

Let us listen to the message of Matter through the voice of science. Let us listen to the message of the Spirit through the voice of spirituality. Finally, let us not forget that spirituality is the soul and science is the body. ౨

Science says:
    "I can."
Nature says:
    "I eternally am."

❋

Science and spirituality complement each other.
Science discovers the many in the One.
Spirituality reveals the One in the many.

Science is that precious thing on earth which is pushed forward by a glowing imagination and pulled forward by its own growing experience. Spirituality is that precious thing on earth which is carried within by fulfilling aspiration and later brought to the fore, where it can become consciously one with God the field of experience, God the experience and God the experiencer.

Within our living memory, we have seen science advancing very fast, while human happiness has been receding at an alarming rate. Today's world is seeing a flickering candle-flame of spirituality, but tomorrow's world will be flooded with the light of spirituality. This is destined and decreed. ෴

A scientist uses the strength of imagination-reality. Imagination is a reality in its own plane, but we do not believe in it until we see it manifested on the physical plane with our ordinary, naked human eyes. The scientist often goes to the intuitive world also, which is one step higher. He enters into the subtle worlds and brings forward their capacity; his discovery has a physical shape, but its real essence comes from the imagination-world or the intuitive world. He may think that he has used his mind, but it is a reality in subtle form that he has brought into physical form, in its own way.

So the scientist will have access to imaginative or intuitive worlds, but even the scientist has to surrender to spirituality, since spirituality houses everything, including science. What the great spiritual giants have achieved in the march of evolution is far beyond the imagination of the scientist. Their spiritual discoveries are not yet possible for the scientist to accept, so he denies them. The scientist wants constant proof on the physical, vital and mental plane, and he does not give value to the spiritual life.

Spirituality will say to science: "I come from a very far-off land, which is totally pure and absolutely authentic. As the physical plane is real to you, even so, the spiritual plane is real to me. Why do I have to prove my achievement by coming down to your level? If I try to prove my achievement to you on a mental level, then instead of giving you illumination, I will only add more confusion to your life. Your scientific discoveries will not and cannot give you abiding satisfaction."

Politics and science are both trying to operate on a particular level, and both are correct according to their own standards. According to their own level of evolution, each is trying to tell the world how creation has to be accepted. Spirituality also tries to offer its truth. It says, "I do not want to explain. Become one and then enjoy." In politics and science you have to prove your capacity, but in spirituality it is not necessary because you become what you achieve. The politician can give a most wonderful speech to the nation, but there may be a vast gulf between the consciousness of the speech and the reality of his life. In his life he does not remain in that kind of elevated consciousness. The scientist may go to a very high intuitive world to discover a great invention, but he does not remain on that plane or even have free access to it. In politics and science, you can claim whatever you have created as your own, but you do not become inseparably one with it. There is always a gap between you and your achievement. In spirituality, however, whatever you realise on the spiritual plane, you become. ॐ

Perfection will dawn here on earth only when the man of prayer and the man of science can establish a genuine friendship and walk side by side towards the self-same goal: humanity's happiness, humanity's satisfaction and humanity's fulfilment both in the inner world and in the outer world. If both the worlds are not happy at the same time, there will always be a tug-of-war between the world within and the world without. ॐ

Science and spirituality must be united. They need each other. Without the one, the other is incomplete, almost meaningless. Together they are not only supremely complete but also divinely meaningful. ॐ

Science likes faultless exactitude.
Nature likes breathless sanctitude.

❊

Man relies on Science.
God relies on Nature.

Why has technology progressed so much in the past fifty years?

The human mind has an instinctive urge to manifest the reality that it embodies as fast as possible, and it has discovered that technology is the fastest means for manifesting this reality. The human mind finds it very easy to manifest itself powerfully and dramatically through technology. At its present stage of development, technology is the best means to carry its messages or to carry the reality and truth that it has already achieved. But technological progress has nothing to do with spiritual progress. It is the mental, vital and physical consciousness that is responsible for technological and mechanical progress. Again, if you compare the soul's progress with the progress of technology, there is no comparison.

If technological improvements give us some material comfort, if they create good circumstances surrounding us, then they may help us in our inner quest. But sometimes when the circumstances around us are better, our aspiration is ruined. When all the world's comforts are there, then instead of meditating and praying, we sleep. If technology brings too much comfort and pleasure to our life, it can be destructive.

We need not lead an austere life; a moderate degree of technology can be of great help to us in our life of acceptance. We can take as much help as we need from technology. But when it is a matter of the soul's reality, the soul's achievement — when it is a matter of light, peace and all the spiritual things that we are crying for — then technology cannot do anything. No matter how fast or how far technology has evolved and developed, it will be of no avail in bringing forward the soul's light or gaining anything from Above. ༅

Science is revolution.
Nature is evolution.

❀

Science is
Prone to theory.
Nature is
Prone to practice.

Is technology acting as a hindrance to spiritual growth?

The answer is in the affirmative as well as in the negative. When modern technology serves as an expression of the inner soul, when it feels that it has a connecting link with the inner life, the inner existence, at that time technology is a help to God-realisation. But very often we see that technology and the inner life do not go together. The outer world with its success is running towards a different goal. We have to be very careful about this, for no matter how much success we derive from technology, the infinite fulfilment cannot take place if the soul is not there. Again, the soul is lame if the outer life does not keep pace with it through technological and scientific progress.

Science and spirituality have to go together, either today or in the distant future. Now they are at daggers drawn. But for the absolute fulfilment of God's Vision and Reality here on earth, science and spirituality must go together. From spirituality we can expect liberation and realisation. From technology and science we can expect material perfection — the material embodiment of the highest Truth. When realisation is inside material success, only then will the material world achieve permanence in eternal values. Again, if perfection is lacking in the inner world, then the material success has to inspire the inner realisation to come and take the lead. ౿

Science has achieved marvels. Nevertheless, its range of vision is limited. There are worlds beyond the senses; there are hidden mysteries. Science has no access to these worlds; science can never solve these mysteries. But a spiritual figure with his inner vision can easily enter into these worlds and fathom these mysteries. Yet a spiritual figure is a real idealist who does not build castles in the air, but rather has his feet firmly planted on the ground. ౿

*The mysteries
Of Mother Nature
None can explain.*

What are the limitations of science and technology?

Science and technology are in the mind. Anything that is in the mind right now is limited because the human mind is not trying to consciously expand or enlarge itself. There are minds that are extremely illumined or illumining, but these minds are rarely to be found on earth. On the whole, the mind that we live in is ordinary. It is full of doubt, fear, anxiety and worry — full of limitations. Since science is in the mind, then definitely these limitations are visible, for science is constantly doubting its own creation or doubting its own achievements.

If we live in the heart, it is all constant self-expansion. The heart is like a divine child looking at the rising sun early in the morning. It receives light in abundant measure. The limitation of science and technology is their incapacity to receive infinite light from Above because they are bound by the mind, which is quite often confused and self-contradictory.

Science is at times known
And at times unknown.
Nature is always
Unknowable.

✹

The mind
Worships science
Because it is powerful.
The heart
Worships Nature
Because it is God-full.

Science thinks
That it knows everything.
Nature feels
That God has given her everything.

✻

Science is
What man's mind has.
Nature is
What God's Heart is.

✻

Science has given humankind
Countless treasure-gifts
And will continue to do so
In the ever-approaching future.

Nowadays people are doing things like grafting flowers to other flowers to create new forms. Is this done by God through man or is it something that God is merely tolerating?

I personally feel that it is God's tolerance. According to me, Nature's pristine beauty disappears when people change the colour of the flower and do all kinds of other things to it. I do not feel that God is working in and through man at that time. God wants to keep Nature's beauty in perfect condition, in its own natural way. But man finds that it is necessary to add to Nature's beauty. Most of the time, we do not add anything to Nature's beauty.

Nature's spontaneous beauty is absolutely the best thing. By adding to it from our fertile brain, the human in us may appreciate the result, but the divine in us may not be able to appreciate it. The natural beauty of a flower God will appreciate. But by adding foreign beauty to this natural beauty, you are taking away almost the life-breath of the flower itself. ζ‐

Anything against Nature is against God. Nature is God the Mother. So if you violate the rules and principles of God the Mother, then how can God the Father tolerate it? He becomes very sad and disappointed when Nature's rules are violated in any way. ⮂

Anything that is simple is real, and anything that is real is progressive. Water, air and everything that is around us in Nature are very simple, but unfortunately what we are doing in our day-to-day life is creating pollution and so many things that are unnatural. In order to exhibit our capacities, we have become unnatural. But if we depend on natural sources, natural things, for example, on our heart, then at every moment we can derive satisfaction, which we are all longing for. ⮂

Science longs
For matter's prosperity.
Nature longs
For beauty's universality.

Science is
Complexity's seriousness.
Nature is
Simplicity's sweetness.

Science is
Man's mind-experience.
Nature is
God's Life-Proclamation.

❄

Science is always in a hurry.
Nature has Eternity
At her disposal.

*F*rom God's point of view,
*E*ach creation of His
    Is absolutely sacred.

A Philosophy of Nature:
The Oneness of Creation

THE EARTH REPRESENTS the Mother aspect of the Divine. It is on earth that Matter and Spirit will find their absolute fulfilment through their reciprocal help and complete union. Matter will see through the eye of the Spirit's vision. Spirit will flower by awakening and energising Matter to become a perfect basis of physical immortality and human transformation on earth. The two main characteristics of the soul of the earth are aspiration and compassionate tolerance.

The earth has a consciousness. It is the consciousness of constant self-giving. The earth is crying and crying for the Infinite, and at the same time offering itself to the Infinite. ࿐

We all know Charles Darwin's theory of evolution, the evolution of species. It is the change in the physical organism from lower to higher, or from simpler to more complex. Spiritual evolution runs parallel to physical evolution. The soul exists in all beings. True, it is divine and immortal, but it has its own urge to be more complete, more fulfilling and more divine. Hence in the process of its evolution, it has to pass from the least perfect body to the most perfect body. Meanwhile it takes into itself the real value of all its earthly experiences. Thus the soul grows, enriching itself, making its divinity more integral, more harmonious and more perfect. ࿐

Creation continuously renews itself and, at the same time, it is in constant evolution. Creation is evolving; that is to say, God is evolving in and through His own creation. In our own life we make constant progress, which is our gradual transformation. So in God's creation we see constant transformation, we see gradual progress. 🌿

❋

In His transcendental aspect,
God is the Lord of Nature.
In His universal aspect,
God is Nature itself.

God relies on
This tiny earth-planet
For the manifestation
Of His Transcendental Vision.

❁

Unity in multiplicity
Has always been the plan
Of Mother Nature.

❁

God is Nature's highest quality.
Nature is God's largest quantity.

*N*ature
*Is nothing short of
God-revelation.*

Why is it that the beauty of Nature gives me such boundless joy?

Precisely because the beauty of Nature is the expression of the One who is all Beauty. Whenever we see something, we see inside that thing the inner presence, the inner consciousness, of its creator. The Creator of Nature is God Himself. He expresses Himself in and through Nature. When we see Nature's beauty, we get overwhelming joy because the Creator and Owner is God. The One who is all Beauty is inside His creation, like a mother's heart is inside her child. A mother's heart cannot be separated from the child's existence. Just because we appreciate, admire, adore and worship the One who is all Beauty, we appreciate His creation as well. Sometimes when we want to see the mother, we get joy just by seeing the child because we have found somebody who is part and parcel of her being. The creation itself is part and parcel of the Creator. Since the Creator is not at our beck and call right now, we are satisfied with the creation. 🐚

What is the essence of Nature's beauty?

The essence of Nature's beauty is the Supreme Light or the Supreme Delight in Nature. Nature itself is not complete. Nature is not the doer. Nature has somebody as its boss, and that is the Absolute Supreme. Nature is God's creation. Again, the Creator is inside the creation. That is why we can say that Nature itself is God. But we have to know that it was not Nature who was the Creator. The Creator was above, and after creating He became one with His creation.

I write a poem. Because of my inspiration, aspiration, capacity and dedication, I feel that it is a part of me. The poet and the poem are inseparably one. At that time you can say it is my poem or you can say it is my consciousness. It is the same. Similarly, Nature is God's creation and it also embodies God's Consciousness. That is why we can easily say that Nature and God are one. Nature functions as a representative of God Himself. But we have to know that Nature is aware of the fact that there is somebody inside it who is regulating it. If that portion of the Creator which is in Nature is taken away, immediately Nature becomes lifeless. ꙮ

*G*od speaks to me
Through Nature's beauty.

Nature lives
  Only to reveal
God's Beauty.

❊

Somewhere the world can see God's Beauty —
True, but where?
  In the silence of Nature.

God Is Everything

To me, God is not only the most beautiful Golden Being or Spirit; to me, God is everything. Anything that is God's creation embodies God. Anything that can be seen in God's creation is of God and for God. Anything that you appreciate here on earth is not only an embodiment of God but God Himself.

When we think of God in Heaven, we have more faith in Him. But God is also here on earth — inside me, inside you, inside everyone. God can be Above in any form, or formless, as infinite Light, infinite Peace, infinite Bliss. Again, He can be inside our hearts, where our real existence is. And if we open our eyes and look at Nature, at the mountains and rivers, that also is God.

So no matter which way we appreciate the reality or want to identify ourselves with the reality, we have to feel that we are appreciating and identifying ourselves with

Divinity; and this Divinity we call either God or Spirit or Being. If you do not want to call it God, you are at perfect liberty not to do so. But you have to call it happiness. Happiness itself is God. You can appreciate the beauty of Nature and if you are happy, then the happiness that you are getting is God. In one word, if God has to be defined, then I wish to say God is happiness.

You can forget the word 'God' and say 'Truth'. One of India's great politicians and saints, Mahatma Gandhi, said: "If you say 'God', immediately some people will object to the conception; but if you speak of 'Truth', everybody agrees with you." So if I speak of Truth, boundless Truth inside Nature, then I am satisfied, because this Truth is giving me happiness. So anything that gives one happiness is God. It can be Nature; it can be a personal being and also an impersonal being. God is everything.

Mother Nature is so compassionate!
She shows us how to aspire
For the Highest
Unconditionally.

❊

God's Presence
Can be found very vividly
At the heart-door
Of Mother Earth.

❊

Nature, unlike human beings,
Obeys God implicitly.

Mother Earth, We Bow to You

*For Earth Day 1975, celebrated on 21 March in
New York's Battery Park, the Earth Day Committee
invited Sri Chinmoy to open the programme with a
silent meditation and a short inspirational talk.*

❋

Mother Earth, Mother, we bow to you. We see you with our
searching eyes. You see us, your children, with your glowing
soul and flowing heart.

We love you with our heart's feeble capacity. You love
us with your life's all-embracing reality.

Mother Earth, you are God's Sacrifice-tree. You are
God's Realisation-flower. You are God's Perfection-fruit.

You are beauty's inspiration and duty's aspiration. You
are inspiring God's entire creation to be beautiful, soulful

and fruitful. You are aspiring in and through God's universe for God-satisfaction in God's own way.

God blesses you constantly with His universal Delight and His transcendental Pride because you teach your children that transformation of human nature and not extinction of human nature is God's supreme choice.

God loves you most. Why? Because you love Him only. Because you suffer for Him only. Because you prosper for Him only. Because you have taught yourself that His choice is your choice, His voice is your voice. You have no choice of your own; you have no voice of your own. Your eternally and unconditionally surrendered oneness is your perfection-cry and God's Satisfaction-Smile.

You are at once God's Silence-creation and His Sound-creation. With your sound-might you tell us, your children, how divinely great God is. With your silence-height you tell us, your children, how supremely good God is. You also tell us that God's universal Greatness we eventually will become and that God's transcendental Goodness we sempiternally are.

Mother Earth, powerfully you concentrate, soulfully you meditate, fruitfully you contemplate. In your concentration we see God the infinitesimal atom. In your meditation we see God the ever-expanding Infinity. In your contemplation we see God the Beloved Supreme. In the inner world you are God's confidence in Himself. In the outer world you are God's assurance to Himself. God is your teacher. God is our teacher. He has taught you how to give to us unconditionally. He has taught us how to receive from you soulfully. The teacher says that you have done extremely well in the examination, while we have sadly failed. Therefore, Mother Earth, we congratulate you, we admire you, we adore you. Mother Earth, Mother, to you we bow and bow.

Meditation: The Joy of the Rising Sun

For newness, meditate on the rising sun. Although it is the same sun that is rising, every day we can see a new beauty inside the sun. Our mind is telling us that it is the same sun that we saw yesterday and the day before yesterday. But when the heart sees this same sun, there is tremendous joy, tremendous thrill, tremendous ecstasy. The mind will not care to look at the rising sun because the mind feels that it is the same old thing. But the heart eagerly says, "When will it come? When will it come? When will it come?" We have to see and feel everything with the heart, not with the mind. If we use the heart, then everything is new. Every day, even though we are doing and seeing the same thing outwardly, the heart is constantly feeling new joy.

My morning begins
With the hope of enjoying
The exquisite beauty of God the creation.

❀

The rising sun and the setting sun
Inspire my heart to become one
With Mother Nature.

God's Love
   For each and every creation of His
   Is not only unbounded
   But also inexhaustible.

※

   God's Way:
      God loves
      Not only human beings
      But His entire creation
      Every day more and more.

My consciousness dances
With boundless sky and air.
It also sports with the waves of the sea.
And I am on the top of the mountain peak.
No place there is on earth
Where my consciousness is not.
I am offering my self-form
To the service of the Absolute Supreme.

*H*ope knows no fear.
Hope dares to blossom
Even inside the abysmal abyss.

Inside hope there is power.

Epilogue:
The Power of Hope

Now that a spiritual awakening is upon the world, it is only a question of years — and certainly not centuries — before its golden glint falls on the face of every nation. The Divinity now hidden beneath the surface will shine forth, to a greater or lesser degree, upon each one.

We are all God's creation. He will not allow His creation to be destroyed – never, never! For years we have been going through a very dark period. Sometimes we know that when the night is the thickest, then the bright dawn appears. Right now the world situation is most deplorable. But this is not going to last for good.

As a God-seeker and God-lover, I feel that very soon – I am not saying tomorrow, or in a month or year or two, but in the near future – a new light will dawn, and it will clear all the thick clouds that have gathered for years. So it is not what we are saying now, not what we are doing now, but what we will ultimately become that matters. We will ultimately become choice instruments of God.

Our philosophy is hope. Hope is not a kind of mental hallucination. Inside hope looms large promise, and when we fulfil our promise, then we feel that our inner strength has done it – not the outer strength of destructive weapons, nuclear weapons. No, it is our heart's inner strength, the strength of oneness. ༀ

A sleepless oneness-heart
Is the only thing
That the world badly needs.

❋

God is proud of us
Only when we do not give up
The hope of becoming
Good citizens of the world.

❋

We must create
A new world of beauty
Here in this world of thorns.

There must be a great synthesis between the inner life and the outer life. The inner life wants love, and the outer life wants power. Now we are all exercising the love of power. But a day will come when this world of ours will be inundated with the power that loves. Only the power that loves can change the world. ⌒

※

I do not give up,
I never give up,
For there is nothing
  In this entire world
That is irrevocably unchangeable.

God says that
At His choice Hour
He will take care
Of the world's problems.

❄

This earth-planet
Is destined to reveal
God's celestial Beauty
Throughout the length and breadth
Of the world.

❄

Nature's last message to mankind:
Do not mistreat me!
If you mistreat me,
You will be a deplorable loser
In the battlefield of life.

As the countless drops
Of the boundless ocean
Or the myriad leaves
Of a huge banyan tree
Peacefully remain side by side,
Even so, all human beings
Will someday live side by side
In a perfect oneness-world.

There shall come a time
when this world of ours
will be flooded with peace.
Who will bring about this radical change?
It will be you —
you and your sisters and brothers.
You and your oneness-heart
will spread peace
throughout the length
and breadth of the world.

SOURCES

Most of the texts in this volume can be found in their original context by searching on *srichinmoylibrary.com*. They have been excerpted from Sri Chinmoy's more than 1600 books, including the following.

A Galaxy of Beauty's Stars
A God-Lover's Earth-Heaven-Life
A Peace-Collecting Pilgrim-Soul
A Soulful Cry Versus a Fruitful Smile
Aspiration-Glow and Dedication-Flow
Consciousness: God-Journey to Man, Man-Journey to God
Conversations with Sri Chinmoy
Earth's Cry Meets Heaven's Smile
Eastern Light for the Western Mind

Secrets of the Inner World
Seventy-Seven Thousand Service-Trees
Simplicity, Sincerity, Purity and Divinity
Something, Somehow, Somewhere, Someday
Songs of the Soul
Soul-Education for the Family-World
Sri Chinmoy Answers
Supreme, I Sing Only for You
Ten Thousand Flower-Flames
The Caged Bird and the Uncaged Bird
The God of the Mind
The Heart-Tears of a God-Seeker
The Summits of God-Life: Samadhi and Siddhi
The Vision of God's Dawn
Twenty-Seven Thousand Aspiration-Plants
World-Destruction: Never, Impossible!
Yoga and the Spiritual Life: The Journey of India's Soul

ABOUT THE AUTHOR

Sri Chinmoy was born in the village of Shakpura in the East Bengal region of India (now Bangladesh) on 27 August 1931. He had a simple, idyllic upbringing, nurtured by his loving parents and six older brothers and sisters. He was also surrounded by great natural beauty, as he roamed among lush green rice paddies, climbed mango trees and explored the nearby forests.

When Sri Chinmoy was eleven, his father passed away followed within a year by his mother, abruptly exposing the young boy to deep sorrow. With his brothers and sisters, he went to join his eldest brother who had taken up residence in the Sri Aurobindo Ashram in South India. The Ashram was the epicentre of a spiritual and cultural renaissance led by Sri Aurobindo, the renowned mystic and philosopher who had been a revolutionary for Indian independence.

It was in this community that the young boy's heartfelt aspiration to understand the essence of human existence was fulfilled through profound meditative experiences of the Infinite. His deep inner realisations of humanity's unlimited capacity and the oneness of all creation with the Supreme led Sri Chinmoy inward in a journey of blissful self-discovery, where he would remain absorbed in meditation and contemplation for many hours each day.

Rather than advocate escape from life, the Ashram encouraged an integral spirituality including service and cultural activities as well as physical fitness. Sri Chinmoy excelled there as a champion sprinter and decathlete, and was appreciated as a blossoming poet and musician.

In 1964, heeding an inner call to share his inner realisation with Western seekers, Sri Chinmoy came at the age of 32 to live in New York City, where he worked at the Indian Consulate for several years.

Over the next four decades, Sri Chinmoy's life of service blossomed. In 1970 he began offering non-denominational peace meditations at the United Nations, at the invitation of

Secretary-General U Thant. As he met to share inspiration with many dignitaries and seekers, he responded to their concerns and questions about current issues, including the environmental crisis, offering his perspective on humanity's relationship with the natural world. He became friends with a number of global peace leaders, including Mikhail Gorbachev, Nelson Mandela, Mother Theresa and Desmond Tutu, and met with prominent environmental advocates such as Maurice Strong, Jane Goodall and Arne Naess (*see photos below*).

Always seeking innovative pathways to peace, he offered over 700 free musical concerts for peace, and established the Sri Chinmoy Oneness-Home Peace Run, a global torch relay that has traversed over 160 countries, with over 5 million students, citizens and government officials participating.

A highly prolific author, composer and artist, Sri Chinmoy wrote over 120,000 poems and published more than 1,500 literary works, including prose, poetry, plays and lectures he gave at the United Nations and major universities worldwide. He strived through his creative work to illumine the heart and to lift the audience above the trials and tribulations of life.

His poems range from lyrical works in the devotional tradition of Bengal, to brief two-line aphorisms, often compared to ancient Sanskrit sutras in the depth conveyed with disarming simplicity.

Sri Chinmoy received a number of honorary doctorate degrees, as well as numerous accolades and citations from universities and cultural organisations around the world.

He passed away on 11 October 2007 at his home in New York City. The Sri Chinmoy Centre carries on his work, striving to promote a culture of peace and to serve the world in accordance with its founder's timeless teachings. ❧

Maurice Strong receives the U Thant Peace Award from Sri Chinmoy on 2 May 1996, at the Church Center for the United Nations, in New York. The two also met on 25 February 1992, when Mr. Strong was serving as the Secretary-General of the 1992 UN Conference on Environment and Development (Earth Summit). Mr. Strong had also been Secretary-General of the 1972 UN Conference on the Human Environment and the first Executive Director of the UN Environment Programme.

After years of corresponding, Sri Chinmoy met with Professor Arne Naess, the Norwegian philosopher, and his wife Kit-Fai Tsui in Oslo, where they were Guests of Honour at Sri Chinmoy's Peace Concert at the Nobel Institute on 30 April 2007. Professor Naess is considered the founder of deep ecology.

Dr. Jane Goodall, renowned primatologist, environmental advocate and UN Messenger of Peace, met with Sri Chinmoy on 18 April 2003 in New York, where she received the Lifting Up the World with a Oneness-Heart Award. Sri Chinmoy called her "a supreme messenger of peace and hope." He added, "With hope we are still alive, and with hope we shall be able to fulfil our promise ... of a oneness-world."

Sri Chinmoy opens the programme for Earth Day 1975, celebrated on 21 March in New York's Battery Park, with a silent meditation and a short inspirational talk, at the invitation of the Earth Day Committee.

OTHER WORKS BY SRI CHINMOY

Meditation

This book, presented with simplicity and clarity, will take you
from the beginning stages of concentration and meditation through
the advanced practice of contemplation and higher states of consciousness. Sri Chinmoy's writings belong to the ancient stream
of wisdom that elevates meditation to the sacred and restores its
deeper purpose of spiritual awakening and self-knowledge.

The Jewels of Happiness

This treasure chest of wisdom features insightful commentary,
useful visualisation exercises, and uplifting aphorisms and poetry
by Sri Chinmoy, with chapters on peace, simplicity, enthusiasm
and other keys to a fulfilling life. *The Jewels of Happiness* now
comes with a free audio book with chapters read by luminaries
such as Nobel Peace Laureate Archbishop Desmond Tutu, singer
Roberta Flack, Olympic legend Carl Lewis, actress Judith Light
and Russian singer Boris Grebenshikov.

The Wings of Joy

This popular volume includes inspirational parables, anecdotes, advice and poems by Sri Chinmoy, on how to cultivate positive qualities in our life and transform fear, anxiety and other challenges. Published by Simon & Schuster, over 100,000 copies have been sold worldwide.

Flute Music for Meditation (CD)

While in a state of profound meditation, Sri Chinmoy plays his haunting melodies on the echo flute. Its rich, soothing tones will take you to the deepest abode of inner peace and harmony. This best-selling recording, an excellent aid to meditation and relaxation, is available from online music sources as well as distributors of Sri Chinmoy's books.

For information about more books and CDs by Sri Chinmoy and how to order them around the world, kindly visit

srichinmoybooks.com

For more information about Sri Chinmoy, his philosophy and his lifetime of service to humanity, please visit

srichinmoy.org

❋

To find out more about Sri Chinmoy's philosophy of Nature and ideas for action, please visit

listentonature.net